욕심을
부리지 않으려 하는 것도
욕심이다

욕심을
부리지 않으려 하는 것도
욕심이다

초판 1쇄 인쇄 2019년 7월 4일
초판 1쇄 발행 2019년 7월 8일

신고번호 제313-2010-376호
등록번호 105-91-58839

발행처 보민출판사
발행인 김국환
편집 정은희
지은이 TEO
디자인 김민정

주소 인천시 서구 불로동 769-4번지 306호
전화 070-8615-7449
사이트 www.bominbook.com

ISBN 978-89-97159-99-4 03800
CIP 2019023822

욕심을
부리지 않으려 하는 것도
욕심이다

TEO 시집

욕심을 부리지 않으려 하는 것도 욕심이다

Missing… is it real

Wind waves tree
Darkness covers mountain
Rain is pouring down
Could find nothing
Nobody hear on me

Falling singing birds
Trampled bug on the ground
Can not breath in the dust
Burning uncontrolled beating sky

Where are you

Try not to desire is desire

선물

Today
Walked to reach you today
Found to give you today

Something different
Special have never seen before
To make you not to forget
To make you never forget

But you didn't come
Left without a word

You didn't come back
Just left without any word

I am still waiting you
Cause could not leave you

Will wait till to day
The day you back

만남

Recognized at a sight
The one my half

Marvelous feeling
Never imagined

Haze memories
A halo of past life

Since met
I am living in other universe
Discovered innovative ecstasy

Pressed button
Becoming another organism
The fantastic dreams are coming true

Praying thanks to god
Doubting if in illusion I am

How wonderful it is
How beautiful you are

첫걸음

Knowing what really I want
Is the most difficult thing

Do not try too big
For the first step
There will be a price for
If you too hurry

Do not sorrow too much
Sometimes should retrace
There will be a price for
Even though you fail

Hesitation, worry, pain, joy
Regret & responsibility
Embrace your friends of the life

Step by step
Further and further

용기

Courage in blood
Wakes me up

See clear blue sky
Feel bounce of heart

Try what you think
As if there is no tomorrow

Fly where you wanna go
As if there is no gravity

But before
Prepare as far as you can
Opportunities are very limited

도전

Throw down the gauntlet
To the champion

The dice was cast
On the ground

Brave man
Get your sword
Advance to the enemies

You have the right
To take it back

Do not be afraid

Rather die
Without begging for a short more life

여름

The time closest to the sun
Oppressive heat kills people

Festival
Trying not to crazy in the heat

Horror films
Trying to feel a flash cool consolation

Ice cream
The most sweet gift from summer

But
First wash your hands
The easiest way to protect you

Also remember
Growing moneys at field
Hotter is better for someone

아기새

Birds wing their way to stay
During the severe winter

A eyas stands on a cliff alone
With wings hidden
With claws concealed

Too young still
Too weak yet but
Flied up to hunt without faltering

Never tried before but
Knows well have to kill at once
No another chance to survive

Instinct controls
Woke up cruel blood

다짐

Pledge my word
Never get back from the enemy
Even though bleed
Even to die

Promise my word
Never betray you my whole life
Love you forever
Even to die

Will be together with you
To the end and always
Even to die
Even to heaven

계획

So many plans have to do
So confusing how to do
So difficult what to do

Start up plan
Short term plan
Long term plan
Business plan
Family plan
Relax plan
Middle age plan
Old age plan
Whole life plan

I rather follow just the way
My heart is flowing away

삶

Cut down legs by axe
Flied hands away by sword
Slashed head over by iron mace

Destroyed body trampled
Under the foot

Drained heart
Stopped beating

As time goes on

Hoped a piece of bread
Wanted to hear children's laugh
Dreamed a nap under waterside tree

But
Stuck in unavoidable pain
Out of controlled exhausted body

Disappearing slowly
Forgotten gradually

사랑

Happened the imagination
Appeared the fantasy

Felt that was love at the first sight
Although never experience before

Embarrassed feeling
Unclear happiness

Drown into deep beauty swamp
Unescapably, irresistibly

Dimly got to know
The reality came into my life

Do not know what to think
Do not know how to behave

가치

Hard to know the worth
Till you lose it

Should realize the worth
Now you have

Look past sometimes
Learn from the mistakes

Dedication is worth
Cannot be measured by money

Kindness is worth
More than beauty

Good speech is worth as silver
But silence is worth as gold

A pound of brave
Can be a ton of luck

백야

In the midnight
The sun is rising again

Seemed like the sun was going to set
But didn’t, rise again, amazing Scandinavia!

As if to vomit the anger of winter
As if to remind the power to the world

Blew out a stream of smoke
Under admire the revived sun on a hotel terrace

술

One of greatest invention of human
Not a gift from nature

Fascinating liquid
Makes the world softly

Pure water of wisdom
Can be a medicine or a poison

Truth lies at the
Bottom of bottle

Nothing more pleasant
Than drink with old friends

Begins people drink alcohol
Later alcohol drinks alcohol

커피

Instant moment
Immediate reaction

Unknown the causes
Just focus on the situation

Dark clouds hang over around
Gathering all senses on

Exhausted body
Drained blood

Resolved again
Have to accomplish the mission

이별

Woke up
With a terrible hangover

Insecure feeling
Suffered headache
Hard to breathe
Falling tears

But I move to work today again

How can get you away from me
How can get you away from me

To live

추억

Passion
Yes passion

Composite of attractive violent flame
Fascinating sentimental young story

Fell in love at the first sight
Now I cry mere mention the name

Sometimes people want to go back but

Memories are beautiful
When is in memories

봄

Spring pervading to nature
My favorite time of year

Beautiful singing birds
Clothes land with green
Plants push out new shoots
Wanders mind
Blooms flower

Winter was seems to never allow Spring but
At last stopped blowing harsh wind and snowing
Finally it has come

How long was look forward to
But easy to forget how much I was

It comes slowly and goes very faster

People miss Winter as soon as it goes
Forgotten how hard it was

어리석음

Brandish knife to kill mosquito
Burn house to kill bedbug

Disobey against parents
No fraternal with brother

Not follow even if aware it is right
Treat according to benefit

Good man speaks good word
Good word stays in good man

지혜

Age brings wisdom
Wise man takes it from old advice

Good word makes good response
Get greed after look precious thing
Don’t ask which I dislike
Don’t decide by the one side
Don’t be blinded by the lure of sweet
Don’t act too fast, do it after think
Can’t make clap by a hand
Bitter taste good for health
Too much think make worries

문제

Broken all bones
Not stop bleeding heart inside but

Aware well aware
Screamed again and again but

Can't get you out of mind
Can't get you out of sight

Getting falling
Into unescapable trap

Sucking slowly
Dying softly

모순

A spear can break anything
A shield nothing can break

Rich is happy
Poor is unhappy?

Many is good
Nothing is bad?

Existence is valuable
Illusion is useless?

Too much loves could ruin you
Severe pains might grow you

Luck is not forever
Crisis can be a huge chance

See what you see
Know what you know

문제 해결

Measure the situation
Include all the single thing related

The most important thing is
Find real root cause why it happened

Investigate advice from older
You are not the only one have it

Analyze solution
Try to fix it very carefully

Verify the result
Apply the theory to the reality

Resister it in mind
Never repeatable

재회

As like
Reunited dropping water
The other side of magnet
We met again

Do not know
How could breath so far
What else could I ask

Full of brilliant moment
Delight have ever gotten

A supernatural being
The eternal rest

As long as I can
As far as will be with you

격정

Unrestrained aggression
Simmering anger

Dreadful loneliness
Anxious future

Too much knowledge
Brings sorrow

Detour sometimes faster
Enjoy the gift from god

Do not give up

Till you know what you got
Till you see how beautiful the world

겨울

Sun turned mind getting away
Earth goes down into a grief

Bleak days
Frosty wind makes moan
Land stood hard as iron
Water halted like stone
Snow had fallen on snow

If no winter
Spring won't come
Even if it comes
Not be so pleasant

Don't be afraid
Let's take forgotten pleasure
Warm rest at fireside
Happiness in family home
Comforts after work

백일홍

A woman stood on a cliff
Looking down over the sea

There are big waves only
Realized he didn't come finally

Dreamed him return from the voyage
Just wanted to be with him but

Been a hundred days has waited
Without any food even water
Can't be stand any longer

Falling slowly down to the sea
Dropped tears become a flower

여행

Let's take heavy breakfast
It is gonna be tough and long

First expedition to the mars but
Don't be too much excited or feared

Pay attention
Could lost your suitcases

Watch your step
Could roll off from the bridge

If not ready enough you are
Can't appreciate the real magnificent view

결혼

Swear by god only speak the truth
Only one I love from now on and forever

Promise not to bring you regret
The decision until the last day

Felt our previous existence forgotten
Saw the scene of domestic everlasting bliss

Let's make beautiful language
Just for two of us

Let's feel the ripe of revolution
In the our universe

시련

Familiar feeling
Was used to but been a long time
Actually almost forgotten
Have never wanted to meet again

But faced today… again

Tighten loose mind up
Stimulate all nerves
Grind rusty knives

The war is coming

Do not cry and calm down
Clear the most big & urgent thing first
Analyze the reason and extinguish fire

Do not get fear
Be more dignified like you did before

To survive

어머니

The most important one
Loved more than anything
Was me to her

Lived like sacrifice is only her duty
Left like finished spawning salmon

As a disoriented bullet
Can not think how to do

I only gave disappointment but
You never give up and made me twice

More beautiful word can be in the world?
How can I ever repay?

육아

Try to be a best judge
But respect their speaks

You can't be right one hundred percent
Could mistake sometimes

Confess sincerely
If you want to make them sincere

Do not spare the rod if fault
Unless want to spoil them

Incredible
How they make same problems
What I did when I was young… omg

가을

It is in the air
The best season for reading

Snake casts its skin
Deer casts its horn

Leaves are changing their color
Every leaf becomes a unit of the
Great colorful harmony

Indeed
Thankful for the harvest
Crowning glory of the year

It is time
Gathering together for human
Scattering abroad for nature

사회생활

Continuous choice
Fall down once choose wrong

Tough survival game
In the organization

The way
For life unavoidable

But do not get afraid of fail
It is gonna be an experience
Of real world at least

Remember
Balance home life and career
To make good harmony

Ok now you are social man
Enjoy the social life

친구

Missed more than thought
Tough memories of the old days

Familiar path
Fragrant wine

No need word too much
Cause know already each other

It is enough just stand by
But pounded heart with excitement

Let's drink all this night
Feels been a hundred years we met

바다

The sea froths over my feet
A piece of 70% of the planet

Feels, the playing sound
Tastes, my favorite food from
Relaxes, in the peace

It sometimes blue
Calm and joyful

It sometimes gray
Waving as boiling

It sometimes dark
Hit and swallow anything

It is obscure unknown world still but
Rich repository of natural resources

There is a ship sails far out
Sucking the red sun

비주류

Outside of the mainstream
Feels such as sorrow

But nothing lasts forever
Mainstream becomes non-mainstream
Non-mainstream becomes mainstream
As time goes by thing's changing

Don't be so sad
Walk the way as you are

Your time will come soon
Appreciate your real worth someday

포기

Finally, decided to give up
Base on the current situation

Felt sure it is time to do so
Have to say goodbye to the people

But it is not the end
Is a new start

Do not fall into despair
The way is not the only one

Never walk out from you
No matter how difficult it is

Once you run away
You will really get fail

Believe yourself
Can find a new better way very soon

절망

The ashes of despair
Going up in the air by wind

Loveless marriage
Disoriented arrow
Heatless heart
Soulless life

Drove them to
Throw them into

But the conclusion is fool
Too early dumped all hope

Do not give way to despair
Though things went against you

Do not know the last scene
Nobody knows how it is going

중년

A greedy man

Seems to live like mice
Tend to staying in unreasonable annoying

Crumbling mountain
Fading dreams
Unconscious purpose

Led by responsibility
Keeping blooming sprout

Becoming an old man

내려놓음

A creation of desire
It is time to put down

The newspaper, phone, pen
No need any more put them down
On the table with your desire

And now it is time to get
Peace, relax, rest, break
Vitalizing your body agonized

Do not hesitate
You are deserve to take

Enjoy this moment
Of the real comfort

아들

I remember
The first moment we met
The heart worried but excited

Was looking for
Proper way to teach

Made a name to make you
Truly sincerely really

Fantastic amazing gorgeous
No word can show enough in the world my son

I love you

가족

Believe without doubt
Happiness spend time with
Provide place to relax
Send everlasting love
Support endless effort
Embrace all the fault
Sacrifice without price
Understand all the mistakes
Await for me always

회상

Time flows
Memories of childhood
Stormy passions of youth
Various experiences of manhood

A light the end of the tunnel
No gains without pains

Believed the belief
Tried to be a rolling stone

Life is only one
Did best all can do?

It is not finished yet
It is time for last spurt

Let's not make any regret
When we close eyes

심플

The best solution is simple
Difficult solution makes confusion

The best food is simple
Basic taste makes deep howling

Language of truth is simple
Moves people's mind

Real friend is simple
Same all the time

가르침

Be sincere
It will be come out on the world very soon

Face the truth
Nothing really matter actually

Don’t be mean to the weak
It will retrace to you someday

Try to sit by good person
The climate to be influenced

Hope not regret
Due to ignorance of it

아버지

I was being without aware
The one who made me standing
Farther always

Have never interested
Just complained of my lack

Now I am standing
Farther from
The one who I made love above all

Remember the face look
Now I see it on my face

평화

In the peace has made
By enormous weapon unstably

Only the just man enjoys
The peace just his own

The day of absolute peace
Will see weaker's smile

The last moment of closing eyes
Will feel peaceful and abundant

깨달음

Disappeared and reborn
I am not the one who I was

Leaved nothing
But it is all thing

Saw nothing
But knows everything

Live empty mind
Like blowing winds

Live without greed
Like standing trees

Finally encountered
The endless peace

죽음

Birth
Is the begins of death
Riding on the journey to die

Life
Is not forever
Was rented like your house

Time
Goes to the last journey
Do not have to hurt your heart

Eternal rest
Freed from worries, fears, pains

Finally
Indeed

시

Got feelings in mind
Builds up inside over and over

Becomes something that
Want to express day by day

Gathering the expressions inside
It becomes a poem one day

Compose a poem
Is not a creative writing work for me
Is a careful observation of me